In Case I Haven't Told You...

Randi Sessums

BookLeaf Publishing

India | USA | UK

In Case I Haven't Told You... © 2022 Randi Sessums

All rights reserved.

No part of this publication may be reproduced, stored in a retrieval system, or transmitted, in any form or by any means, electronic, mechanical, photocopying, recording or otherwise, without the prior written permission of the presenters.

Randi Sessums asserts the moral right to be identified as author of this work.

Presentation by *BookLeaf Publishing*

Web: www.bookleafpub.com

E-mail: info@bookleafpub.com

ISBN: 978-93-5744-926-7

First edition 2022

DEDICATION

For my person. You never stop believing in me, so I'll never stop writing.

ACKNOWLEDGEMENT

To every person that gives me something to say; I may not always know how to tell you how I feel or what I'm thinking, so I hope this book gives you a little insight into my head. I'll never be fully able to express out loud what I want to say, but I can always write it. So if you always read it, then you'll know. I wouldn't be where I am without the people who inspired these poems. Whether you drew out my anger, my sadness, or my love, you're the reason I keep writing. Keep rendering me speechless and I'll keep filling the pages.

PREFACE

Let me show you what it feels like to know you. What it feels like to be me. What it feels like to feel, too much. In case I haven't told you, this is what I'm thinking.

Weeds

I used to think our relationship was like a rose,
beautiful, timeless, elegant in nature.
A gesture of intimacy, petals perfect in shape,
meant to be frozen in time or pressed between
the pages of a book.

But the more I think back, the more I realize
it was more like a dandelion.
Growing where it shouldn't, finding a home in
the concrete sidewalk.
Persevering through conditions it wasn't meant
for.

Beautiful at first, but fleeting in the wind.
A delight at first sight, but difficult to get rid of
once you realize they are an infection, spreading
through
a meadow, not fully rooted but refusing to
disperse.

The more you try to remove the dandelions, the
faster their seeds spread. Reminding you, you
can never truly
rid yourself of the fluffy white flower.

Roses are a gift, a blood stain of love and
passion and
everyone wants to capture the rose in a dome,
watch its beauty from behind the glass.

The more I think about it, the more I remember
you,
I realize no matter how much you want it to be a
rose,
a dandelion is still just a weed.

Nail Biting

The tiny pricks appear across the tips of my
nails, evidence of the churning in my stomach.

The world spins through my mind like a hamster
on its wheel

When I say the world, I mean you.

The apprehension on your face as you fiddled
with nothing, like a child afraid of the answer.
"Do you remember everything?"
As if you were testing me, as if you wanted to
know it was just my alter ego who kissed him.
That it wasn't me, it was the tequila that pulled
him to me

Please tell me that one lip locked moment with a
friend isn't enough to push you away

Let me tell you, no, let me show you that he isn't
the one I wanted to kiss that night.
Or any night.
The man I wanted, the man I've always wanted,
the man I still want, left the party early.

I wish you would notice.
You're the only one that left early.

More

Don't let them tell you aren't enough.

You are everything to someone.
You are everything to me.

If you can't believe anything,
Oh honey, I know it's hard to believe
after you've been lied to as much as you have,
but believe this.

They are full of shit.

You are more than enough.

Landyn

The first one is always the hardest,
the first one is always the special one.
You are the first one to hold me in your
gaze and show me that my heart can hold so
much
more, you are the first little hand to wrap around
mine, the first little kiss to grace my cheek
with your first little trust to hold me to
my promises, with your first little life.
A life that is not so little anymore,
but to me you will always be my sweet
little cheese eater who loves to sing and
whose giggle could light a path for anyone to see
the way you are like the first light of sunrise.
You are the first little boy to save me.

Toxicity in My Blood

Worthless
Ignorant Bitch
No man will ever love you
Stupid Liberal
You don't actually care about him
You should have just stayed home
Just after Daddy's money
Hefty girl
Your education means nothing
Daddy issues

Was I meant to forget what you said?

Questions for JJ

Would it matter if you knew how I think about you?

Would it matter if I told you the only way to survive a night with a stranger was to fill my mind with thoughts of you?

Would you think me crazy, or obsessed?

Would you run from me in fear of the emotion I display, or the potential to feel?

Would it matter if I told you I have my own tools, but I choose not to bring them? One tiny excuse to have another stolen moment with you.

If you knew how fast my heart beats when you wear your jeans, would it change how you see me in mine?

If I told you how happy it makes me to see your smile, your old and your new one, would you feel the same?

Do you feel anything?

Would it make me feel better to know, to really
know, how you feel, how you think of me, *if* you
think of me?

Or would I be breaking my own heart? Again.

Am I breaking it by not telling you?

Question after question with no
answers.
Questions with no voice, no intentions, no
expressions.

Questions.

Would it matter if you knew how I feel about
you?

Backseat Breakdowns

Sometimes we have to pray they don't turn the
music down
so they don't hear us crying in the backseat.
The silent sobs that rock through our body, for
every reason and no reason at all.

Sometimes fight or flight whispers in our ear
and we fly.
We fly quickly, no questions asked or answered.
Grab the keys. Shut the car door. Get out before
they notice.

She always notices.

Sobs can't always be silent and
you don't have to be alone to feel lonely.
Tears will always be salty and no matter how far
we turn our head,
they still stream down our faces.

PCOS

What do you do when your body doesn't do
what you want it to do?

Cry
Pray
Keto
Birth Control
Dairy Free
Gluten Free
Exercise
Hope

No one knows what to do or what to say and the
look of pity in their eyes only makes me want
To rip my ovaries out myself and tell them
To work, please work. Please do your job. Please
let me have the one thing I've always wanted.

But don't show yourself too much pity. Even
though there's a reason, there's symptoms,
there's a dysfunction.
If you complain too much, you'll always be the
fat girl who just can't lose weight.

A Hand Through the Dark

Some people say there is no way, no rhyme or
reason for the things that go on.
That things just happen.
Well, if I were to believe that,
then how thankful I would be that you happened
to me.

You came into my life and nothing has been the
same since.
You took my hand and forced me to live, to kiss
the boy, to go to the show, to order the dessert.
You showed me what it's like to be loved,
fearlessly, with no hesitations.
A fierceness that lights up any darkness I see.

You show me that I am worthy of the love that I
wish to receive.
That I am worthy of the good things that happen
to me, and better than the bad.
You turned "I don't know what to do" to "We
can get through it."

You show me that our love languages don't have
to be the same for me to be able to call you at
any time and the first thing you say is "Do you
need me?"

You showed me that soulmates aren't just for
romance.
Soulmates are who we feel most at peace with.
A home within another heart.
And I happen to feel at home in yours.

Petals by Day

The day that I stopped looking at my body as if
it was a prison,
I realized that it was a meadow,
full of beautiful and vibrant flowers.
Peaceful and serene, but still capable of
engulfing you with its power.

The day my body became a vessel
for my soul
instead of a punishment for my thoughts,
was the day I was finally able to invite
someone into my meadow and be comfortable
with them picking a flower.

The day I started to water instead of starve,
the colors have never been the same.

Thorns by Night

No amount of positive body affirmations keep
the cold away
when no one else is around and it's just me,
and the mirror, and the pants that don't fit,
and the reminder of the boys that told me I
wasn't enough.

No amount of fad diets and "lifestyle changes"
make the pit
any smaller when it decides to consume what's
left.
The dark hole that opens in my chest and
reminds me
I'll always be different.

The nagging, shrill voice that insists it's the
folds and
the stretch marks that keep him away.
The voice that sits and waits in the back of my
head,
telling me he would love a size 10 more.

On the Way Down

Sometimes I have to remind myself that the
world is going to fall.
This is okay.
We all have to hurt; we all have to feel things.
If I stop trying to stop it and just spread my
arms, accept the wind,
maybe the landing won't hurt so bad.

And maybe, if I tell myself everyone's world
falls apart sometimes,
maybe I won't feel so alone.

Impressed

The truth is, you don't need shining pearly white
teeth to impress me.

Hold me when the waves crash onto the shore
and threaten to take me with them.
Kiss me when the storms follow me day and
night.
Kiss me in the actual rain.
Honor me in public, disrespect me in private.

You don't need a big paycheck to make me fall
for you.

Be honest when you're upset with me, and open
when you're not.
Tell me what's going on in that cunning brain.
Use your words to seduce me.
Be patient when I'm just as bullheaded as you.
Never stop being as bullheaded as me.
Acknowledge my intelligence.

You don't have to have it all figured out for me
to want you.

Shake my father's hand and show him how you
care for me.
Joke with my brothers.
Bond with my family.
Cuss at me with that sailor's mouth.
Admire my ability to keep up with you.
Show me you respect my intuition.

Let me know you.

You don't have to be perfect.
Just love me like I love you.

Is This Acceptance

No one ever tells you what fear feels like.

Sure, you get scared at killer movies, or when
the boat is too rocky.
A bridge may be too high, or a spider have too
many legs.

But have you ever been afraid of your own
body?
Afraid it won't do the one thing you need it to
do?

Have you ever been afraid of your mind?
Your instincts betraying you, telling you just one
more.

Have you ever been afraid to trust yourself, to
trust the flesh that carries around
the thoughts you can't control,
the impulses you swallow.

Have you ever swallowed the bile as your worst
fear
poked its head into the exam room,
reared its ugly face and taunted:

You were afraid and now look. Your own body is betraying you.

If they would have told me what true, haunting
fear is.
I wouldn't have listened.

The Picture in the Back of the Frame

With its edges worn from the grease
on my fingertips,
pulling it out
Again and
Again and
Again.

Maybe I should have tried harder,
yelled a little louder,
held you while you cried longer.

Maybe I should have been more social.
Gone out drinking every Thursday night,
spun around in my cowboy boots
and hooked up with every guy
who told me he liked
My eyes.

Maybe I should have fought harder,
loved harder,
been your best friend…harder?

Maybe I wasn't good enough or
Maybe YOU weren't good enough.

Maybe you should apologize.
Maybe I should.

Maybe you could be less selfish
or tell less lies,
because maybe the world doesn't revolve around
You.
You and your inability to feel or do anything in
the now.
Your world and your life
and I'm just a pawn.
And maybe you got mad because this pawn
wanted to play
Her own game
and maybe-

Maybe.

I should just throw your picture away.

Plot

If it's not you at the end, I don't want to read this story.

If you aren't the main character, I would like a new book.

If you aren't going to be holding my hand in 50 years, I am skipping this section.

If you aren't meant for me, then why am I in this chapter?

Papa

Amazing grace, how sweet the sound.
The sound of your cough, nestled deep in your
chest
remnants of smoker's lungs peeking through.
Your sweet scent of spearmint and burnt paper,
your leathery hands that are somehow gentle,
but not for everyone. Your maniacal laugh
that shows your missing tooth and the
three hairs that dance on the top of your head,
skin shining through to show the years you have
lived,
and flown, and loved, and I used to listen to you
sing
Gospel songs as the bayou air filled my lungs
and
tangled my hair and while I know your tan skin
will not live forever, I dread the day I won't get
to
hear you sniffle as we say goodbye, one more
time.

In the Case of Fear

I am not afraid of a killer clown, or a
psychopath, or a possessed doll.
I can remember feeling alone and unwanted.

The shadows across the room do not terrify me.
The thoughts of ending up alone do.

The chill in the air doesn't send shivers up my
spine.
The memory of being without does.

The creepy crescendo doesn't make me cover
my eyes.
The fear of never being enough, of them being
right, makes me run and hide.

The only thing that goes bump in the night are
my own thoughts

The Sour Taste of an Opening Procedure

It's the sound the clipboard makes as it lands on my desk, passive aggressively thrown at me.
The sound I hear when your eyebrows shoot too high above your eyes to be telling the truth.
The sound of your sigh, loud enough for everyone to hear, but never vocal enough.

It's the sound of the wooden cylinder crashing across the floor, echoing through my mind.
The sound of blaming everyone but yourself.
The sound of never being the villain, always the victim. I get to be the villain in your voice.

It's the sound of the scream of anger that melts through the walls.
The feeling of walking on eggshells at every turn.
The taste of watered-down coffee as we sit in silence, no one brave enough to approach the dragon's den.

Sounds tumble and draw through my mind,
making it harder and harder to paint the smile,
but
there's the loudest one of all. The one on repeat,
reminding me over and over again
I'm not enough in your eyes.

That's the one that makes the taste of your name
sour in my mouth.

Endings

Endings have a funny way of beginning.

It always starts small. A dish left out for 3 nights, a messy bathroom, a shrugged off effort for connection.

But nothing is ever really that small, is it?

One dish turns into several, laundry to do turns into laundry that's never done, and that spark of intimacy slips farther and farther away every time it's forced.

Little things turn into big things and before either of you know it, the small droplets become the downpour that make you question everything.

Every word, every touch, every thought is put under a microscope, the ant of your relationship burning in the sun of realizations of lost love and self-awareness.

The downpour picks up into a hurricane as friends are asked to choose sides for a war that hasn't even started yet. Battle lines are drawn, preparations are made before both sides know of what's coming.

Decisions are made, no matter the previous intentions. Everyone is hurt in some way, no matter the amount of sugar you pour into the batter.

The hurricane crashes into the shore, no matter how much you want it not to.

Endings don't feel good. They aren't the smiles tinged with sunshine, the promise of right person, wrong time. Endings are painful, and brutal, and necessary. They can be slow and deliberate at an attempt to lessen the blow, or they can be swift and aggressive.

No matter how it is done,

Endings have to end.

Rising Above the Setting

What an interesting world we live in that to end something,
is to begin something else.

Every beginning is beautiful, whether it be scary.
Or easy.
Or hard.
Or necessary.
Or forced.

Things begin, as they end.

We do not always get to choose how they end or how they begin,
but if you could,
would you really want to know?

Would you want to design the life you live,
or would you want to live it?

Remember the sunrise and the sunset contain the same colors, yet we always say one is more beautiful than the other.

Today, choose them both.

www.ingramcontent.com/pod-product-compliance
Lightning Source LLC
LaVergne TN
LVHW010934200726
843509LV00013B/2224